# Letter to Santa Claus

The **FUNNIEST** present I ever received was:

_____

If I was only allowed **ONE** present this year, it would be:

_____

SANTA'S POST BOX
wish lists and postcards only!

Write a letter to Santa to tell him what you'd really like this Christmas!

Dear Santa,

_____
_____
_____
_____
_____
_____
_____
_____

Yours,

The **BEST** present I ever received was:

_____

This year I hope my **DAD** gets:

_____

This year I hope my **MOM** gets:

_____

Count down to Christmas with this handy Advent calendar on the bottom of your placemats! Fill in one a day and keep an eye out for extra placemats along the way.

**24 DAYS TO GO!**

| ① | 2 | 3 | 4 | 5 | 6 | 7 | 8 | 9 | 10 | 11 | 12 | 13 | 14 | 15 | 16 | 17 | 18 | 19 | 20 | 21 | 22 | 23 | 24 | 25 |

# Connect the Gifts

What a mountain of presents! Color them in and count how many there are.

Each house gets as many gifts as it says on their door! Connect each house with the correct pile of gifts.

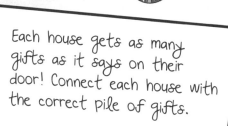
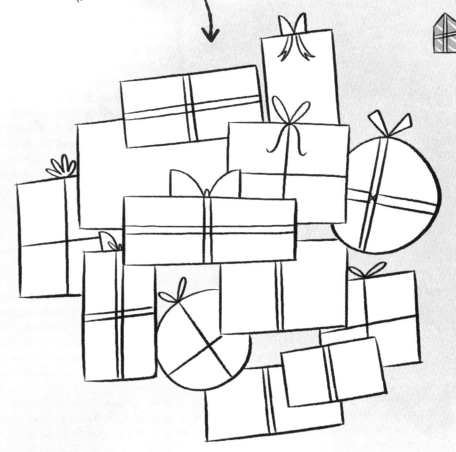

**12**

**5**

**7**

**10**

How many presents? 

**23 DAYS TO GO!**

# What's your christmas style?

Answer the questions to reveal your true Christmas personality!

## ON CHRISTMAS EVE YOU...
A. Go to bed nice and early.
B. Stay up late having fun with your family.
C. Play games and stay awake until really early in the morning because you're too excited to sleep!

## PRESENTS SHOULD BE OPENED...
A. One by one in turn.
B. All at once.
C. As quickly as possible!

## HOW SHOULD YOU DECORATE A CHRISTMAS TREE?
A. Very carefully. It's got to look perfect!
B. Find all your favorite decorations and make sure they all have a place.
C. With LOTS of lights!

## WHAT'S THE PLAN FOR CHRISTMAS DAY?
A. Same as last year! Tradition is very important.
B. Whatever you like! But probably a nap at some point.
C. Presents, food, chocolate, games!

## THE FIRST THING YOU DO WHEN YOU WAKE UP ON CHRISTMAS MORNING IS...
A. Brush your hair. You don't want to look yucky in all those photos!
B. Wait in bed excited, until you hear your family getting up.
C. Run to the living room and start yelling at everyone else to get up!

Color in these gingerbread men!

## ANSWERS:

**MOSTLY As:** Practically perfect! You like Christmas to go as planned with lots of family traditions!

**MOSTLY Bs:** Chilled out! Christmas is a time to have fun and relax. Who cares if the turkey gets burnt or you forget to watch your favorite movie? Pass the chocolates!

**MOSTLY Cs:** Fun, fun, fun! Christmas is a day filled with excitement from the moment you wake up in the morning to the moment your head hits the pillow!

Look out for this symbol on ten extra placemats! You can save them for a rainy day before Christmas, or complete them whenever you want.

# JigsawJumble

Look in the middle to find the missing pieces of the jigsaws! When you find the right piece, draw a line to match it to the correct jigsaw!

Give this picture a **COZY** title!
_____

Give this picture a **FUNNY** title!
_____

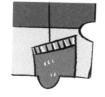

Give this picture a **FESTIVE** title!
_____

Give this picture a **LOVELY** title!
_____

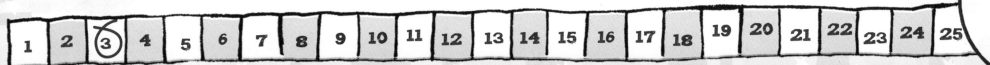

**22 DAYS TO GO!**

# Did You Know

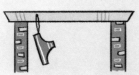

Check out these crazy facts all about Christmas! Watch out, not all of them are correct. Can you figure out which ones are true, and which ones are false?

**1.** In Switzerland, children don't hang Christmas stockings by the fire—they hang up their underwear instead!

True ☐  False ☐

**2.** Turkey wasn't always eaten on Christmas Day in the UK—it used to be a Pig's head!

True ☐  False ☐

Phew!

**3.** In Portugal, places are set at the table for the souls of the dead. Creepy!

True ☐  False ☐

Draw or write about your **SILLIEST** Christmas tradition here!

**4.** Traditional English Christmas Puddings are boiled in a used sock!

True ☐  False ☐

**5.** In Caracas, Venezuela, the streets are closed off on Christmas Day so everyone can roller skate to church.

True ☐  False ☐

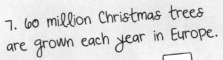

Meow.

**6.** Purple Christmas stockings are bad luck.

True ☐  False ☐

**7.** 60 million Christmas trees are grown each year in Europe.

True ☐  False ☐

1. False, 2. True, 3. True, 4. False, 5. True, 6. False, 7. True.

| 1 | 2 | 3 | ④ | 5 | 6 | 7 | 8 | 9 | 10 | 11 | 12 | 13 | 14 | 15 | 16 | 17 | 18 | 19 | 20 | 21 | 22 | 23 | 24 | 25 |
|---|---|---|---|---|---|---|---|---|----|----|----|----|----|----|----|----|----|----|----|----|----|----|----|----|

## 21 DAYS TO GO!

# Mind Match

Write the first three things that come into your head when you read the words below. Once you have filled them all in, ask your family what words they think of! For each word that matches one of yours, give yourself a point!

## Christmas dinner

1. _____
2. _____
3. _____

SCORE ☐

## Presents

1. _____
2. _____
3. _____

SCORE ☐

## Wrapping paper

1. _____
2. _____
3. _____

SCORE ☐

How many holly leaves can you spot around the page?

_____

## Santa Claus

1. _____
2. _____
3. _____

SCORE ☐

## Tree

1. _____
2. _____
3. _____

SCORE ☐

## Christmas songs

1. _____
2. _____
3. _____

SCORE ☐

Answer: 10.

# Let it Snow!

Color the matching snowflakes with the same color. Then draw some more around them!

Look, it's a **SNOW** globe!

Connect the dots to finish this snowman. Give him a hat and scarf when you're done.

**20 DAYS TO GO!**

| 1 | 2 | 3 | 4 | (5) | 6 | 7 | 8 | 9 | 10 | 11 | 12 | 13 | 14 | 15 | 16 | 17 | 18 | 19 | 20 | 21 | 22 | 23 | 24 | 25 |

# Bauble-tastic

Color in these beautiful baubles and choose your favorite when you're done!

Now color in this bauble following the number code below. Can you see what's inside?

extra

1 = ● Dark brown
2 = ● Light brown
3 = ● Red
4 = ● Green

**19 DAYS TO GO!**

| 1 | 2 | 3 | 4 | 5 | 6 | 7 | 8 | 9 | 10 | 11 | 12 | 13 | 14 | 15 | 16 | 17 | 18 | 19 | 20 | 21 | 22 | 23 | 24 | 25 |

# Find the Difference

Can you find the **EIGHT** differences between these two pictures?

Color in these gifts coming out of the toy factory!

# Handy Angel

Draw an outline around each of your hands to give this angel wings.

Draw faces on these Christmas angels!

Now doodle a pretty pattern on each wing and color in your angel wings!

**18 DAYS TO GO!**

| 1 | 2 | 3 | 4 | 5 | 6 | 7 | 8 | 9 | 10 | 11 | 12 | 13 | 14 | 15 | 16 | 17 | 18 | 19 | 20 | 21 | 22 | 23 | 24 | 25 |

# Oh Christmas Tree

Do you know what each of these leaves are? Connect the correct tree name with its correct leaf!

1     Holly

2     Mistletoe

3     Fir tree

4     Oak tree

Answer: 1. Fir tree, 2. Holly, 3. Oak, 4. Mistletoe

Add some decorations to this tree! You can find some inspiration along the bottom.

Don't forget the angel on top!

**17 DAYS TO GO!**

| 1 | 2 | 3 | 4 | 5 | 6 | 7 | 8 | 9 | 10 | 11 | 12 | 13 | 14 | 15 | 16 | 17 | 18 | 19 | 20 | 21 | 22 | 23 | 24 | 25 |

# Christmas Predictions

How many presents will I get?

_____

(Add up the letters in the month you were born to get your answer.)

What time will I wake up on Christmas morning?

 ____ am (Add two to your age!)

What color will my wrapping paper be?

_____

(The same color as the top you are wearing right now!)

...ZZZZ

Who will fall asleep first after dinner?

_____

(Pretend to sneeze. Whoever says "bless you" first is your answer!)

Who will get the best present?

_____

(Close your eyes for three seconds. Open them, then write down the name of the first person you see.)

Draw yourself on Christmas morning— Pajamas, smile, and all!

How many chocolates will I eat?

_____

(Add up the letters in the day, today. E.g. Wednesday = 9!)

# The Perfect Gift

Use the spaces to draw some amazing gifts that your friends and family would love. Don't forget to write who they are for on the tags!

Use this space to draw your **ULTIMATE**, out-of-this-world present for your best friend!

| 1 | 2 | 3 | 4 | 5 | 6 | 7 | 8 | 9 | 10 | 11 | 12 | 13 | 14 | 15 | 16 | 17 | 18 | 19 | 20 | 21 | 22 | 23 | 24 | 25 |

**16 DAYS TO GO!**

# Christmas Lists

Fill in these lists with all your **FAVORITE** things about Christmas.

My top 3 Christmas games are:

1. _____
2. _____
3. _____

My all-time top Christmas presents were:

1. _____
2. _____
3. _____
4. _____
5. _____

My top 3 Christmas songs are:

1. _____
2. _____
3. _____

My top 10 favorite things about Christmas EVER are:

1. _____
2. _____
3. _____
4. _____
5. _____
6. _____
7. _____
8. _____
9. _____
10. _____

My top 5 favorite Christmas foods are:

1. _____
2. _____
3. _____
4. _____
5. _____

My top 3 favorite Christmas movies are:

1. _____
2. _____
3. _____

The top 3 presents I'd like this year are:

1. _____
2. _____
3. _____

| 1 | 2 | 3 | 4 | 5 | 6 | 7 | 8 | 9 | 10 | 11 | 12 | 13 | 14 | 15 | 16 | 17 | 18 | 19 | 20 | 21 | 22 | 23 | 24 | 25 |

**15 DAYS TO GO!**

# Time to Draw

Use the grids to copy the two pictures square-by-square, or try the snowman freehand. Then color them in!

There are loads of **TOYS** to be made, and Elmer the Elf needs to get to the Toy Factory! Can you help him find the way?

start

Toy Factory

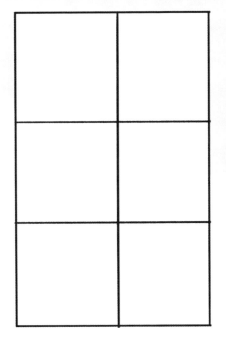
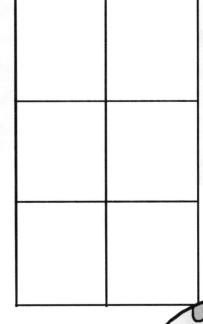

**14 DAYS TO GO!**

# Feeling Festive

Give this plain living room a festive feel!
Color it in and add the decorations.

Add these ornaments
to the tree.

Put a garland around
the fireplace!

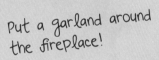

Draw some Christmas
cards on the shelves.

Draw some stockings
hanging from the
mantelpiece.

Copy these shapes if
you're not sure what
else to add!

 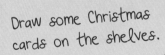 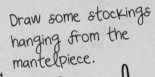  

Place these presents
under the tree!

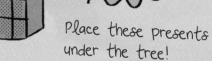

# Which chimney?

Santa needs to find the right chimney to get him to the Christmas tree! Can you help him?

Use crayons and pencils to color in the house. Don't forget to add festive decorations.

**13 DAYS TO GO!**

# It's a Wrap

**NO PEEKING!** Can you guess what these wrapped presents are?

- [ ] Trumpet
- [ ] Guitar
- [ ] Piano

- [ ] Bicycle
- [ ] Boat
- [ ] Car

- [ ] Doll's house
- [ ] Puppy
- [ ] Teddy bear

There's one present missing from Santa's sack! Can you spot which one he has left out? ↗

- [ ] Coat
- [ ] Scarf
- [ ] Mittens

Answer: Blue present: guitar; red present: teddy bear; yellow present: bicycle; green present: mittens

**12 DAYS TO GO!**

| 1 | 2 | 3 | 4 | 5 | 6 | 7 | 8 | 9 | 10 | 11 | 12 | ⑬ | 14 | 15 | 16 | 17 | 18 | 19 | 20 | 21 | 22 | 23 | 24 | 25 |

# Mixed Up

Can you help the elf find his missing present, and the reindeer find his missing carrot?

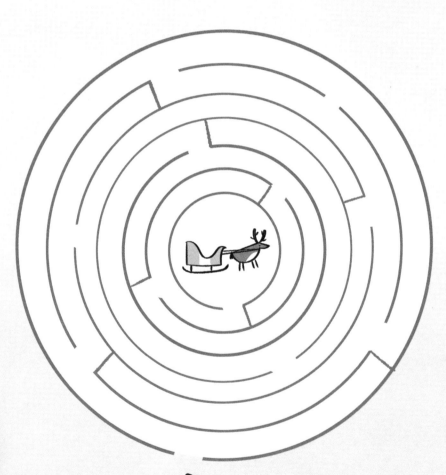

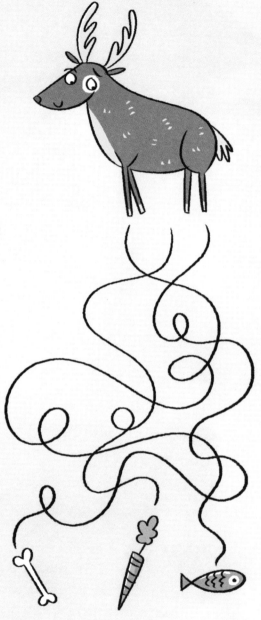

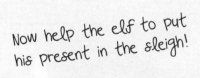
Now help the elf to put his present in the sleigh!

# Reindeer Dash

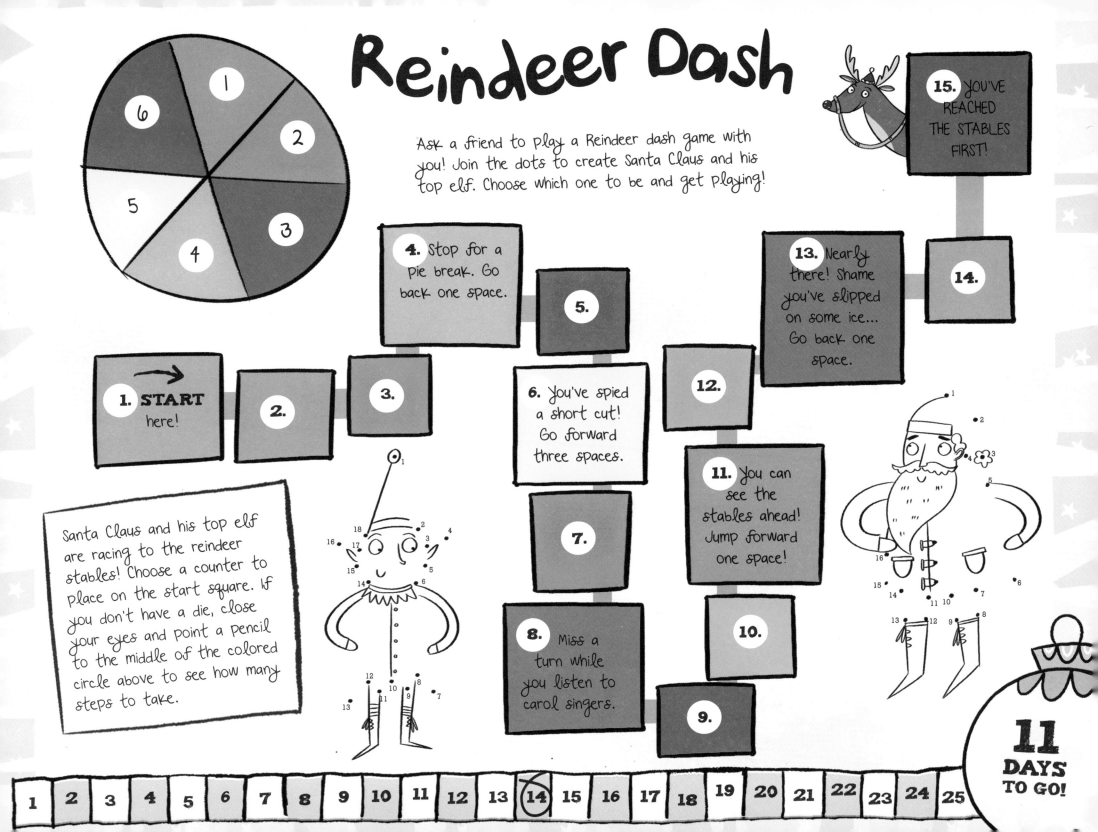

Ask a friend to play a Reindeer dash game with you! Join the dots to create Santa Claus and his top elf. Choose which one to be and get playing!

**15.** YOU'VE REACHED THE STABLES FIRST!

**4.** Stop for a pie break. Go back one space.

**5.**

**13.** Nearly there! Shame you've slipped on some ice... Go back one space.

**14.**

**1. START** here!

**2.**

**3.**

**6.** You've spied a short cut! Go forward three spaces.

**12.**

**11.** You can see the stables ahead! Jump forward one space!

**7.**

Santa Claus and his top elf are racing to the reindeer stables! Choose a counter to place on the start square. If you don't have a die, close your eyes and point a pencil to the middle of the colored circle above to see how many steps to take.

**8.** Miss a turn while you listen to carol singers.

**10.**

**9.**

**11 DAYS TO GO!**

| 1 | 2 | 3 | 4 | 5 | 6 | 7 | 8 | 9 | 10 | 11 | 12 | 13 | 14 | 15 | 16 | 17 | 18 | 19 | 20 | 21 | 22 | 23 | 24 | 25 |

# Memory Fun

How many elves were there?

Take a good look at the pictures in the middle of the mat, then cover them up. Now try and answer all the questions around the outside.

**NO CHEATING!**

What vegetables were on the dinner plate?

How many buttons were on Santa's coat?

How many children were singing carols?

What color was the biggest present under the Christmas tree?

What was the door number on the house?

Who was munching on a carrot?

What was the snowman wearing on his head?

| 1 | 2 | 3 | 4 | 5 | 6 | 7 | 8 | 9 | 10 | 11 | 12 | 13 | 14 | 15 | 16 | 17 | 18 | 19 | 20 | 21 | 22 | 23 | 24 | 25 |

**10 DAYS TO GO!**

# Don't Wake Santa Claus

Santa has nodded off while delivering your presents! Can you tiptoe around him? You can only move forward around the board using the following color sequence: green, yellow, blue, purple.

After you've taken a peek at your gifts, find your way back to bed through the squiggly maze!

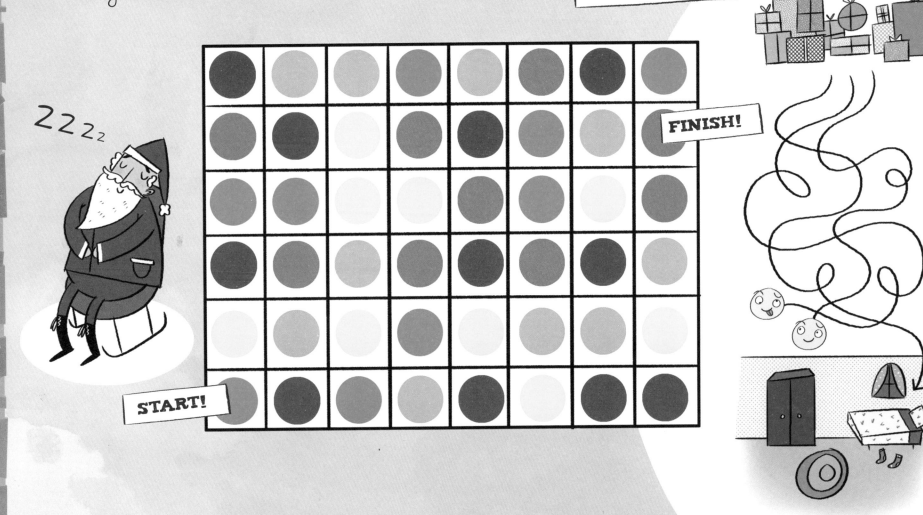

**START!**

**FINISH!**

ZZZz

**9 DAYS TO GO!**

| 1 | 2 | 3 | 4 | 5 | 6 | 7 | 8 | 9 | 10 | 11 | 12 | 13 | 14 | 15 | (16) | 17 | 18 | 19 | 20 | 21 | 22 | 23 | 24 | 25 |

# The Ultimate Christmas

If you could have the Christmas of your dreams, what would it be? Write down your Christmas dreams here.

I would spend my Christmas in this country:

I would have Christmas dinner with this celebrity:

My secret Santa would be:

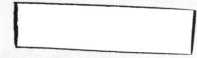

Give Santa the ultimate fashionable Christmas suit!

I would have

for Christmas dinner.

I would wear

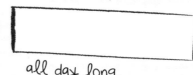

all day long.

I would go to bed at

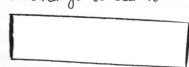

# Mrs. Claus's Bakery

Mrs. Claus likes nothing better than to bake her famous cakes and cookies, but something seems to have gone wrong in her kitchen! Mrs. Claus has forgotten when to add the ingredients in her recipe. Follow the lines to figure it out for her!

Eggs

Butter

Sugar

Flour

Can you find the matching gingerbread men on the other side of the page? Circle them in the same color to match the pairs.

The correct order is: butter, sugar, eggs, and flour!

8 DAYS TO GO!

1 2 3 4 5 6 7 8 9 10 11 12 13 14 15 16 17 18 19 20 21 22 23 24 25

# Puzzle Mania

Create four new elves for Father Christmas's workshop! Start by thinking up a fun elf name, then draw in what they look like.

Color this elf in with funky colors. Maybe try giving him purple shoes and a blue hat!

Welcome to the Christmas Sudoku! You can only have one type of object in each row, column, and mini-square. Place the missing objects in the grid!

**7 DAYS TO GO!**

1 2 3 4 5 6 7 8 9 10 11 12 13 14 15 16 17 ⟨18⟩ 19 20 21 22 23 24 25

# Quick Quiz

See if you can answer these Christmas questions, then make your own quiz in the middle to test your family and friends!

**1. What is a reindeer's favorite snack?**

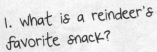

**2. What date is Christmas?**

**3. How many ornaments should you have on your tree?**

1. _____

2. _____

3. _____

4. _____

5. _____

6. _____

7. _____

8. _____

9. _____

10. _____

Now it's **YOUR** turn! Write your own Christmas quiz questions to ask your friends and family. Don't forget to write down the answers too!

**4. What is the last day of Christmas called?**

**5. Apart from an angel, what is traditionally put at the top of a Christmas tree?**

**6. What is the name of the rich and very selfish man in the book "A Christmas Carol" by Charles Dickens?**

# Sleigh Ride

All these presents have a matching pair. Can you find them all?

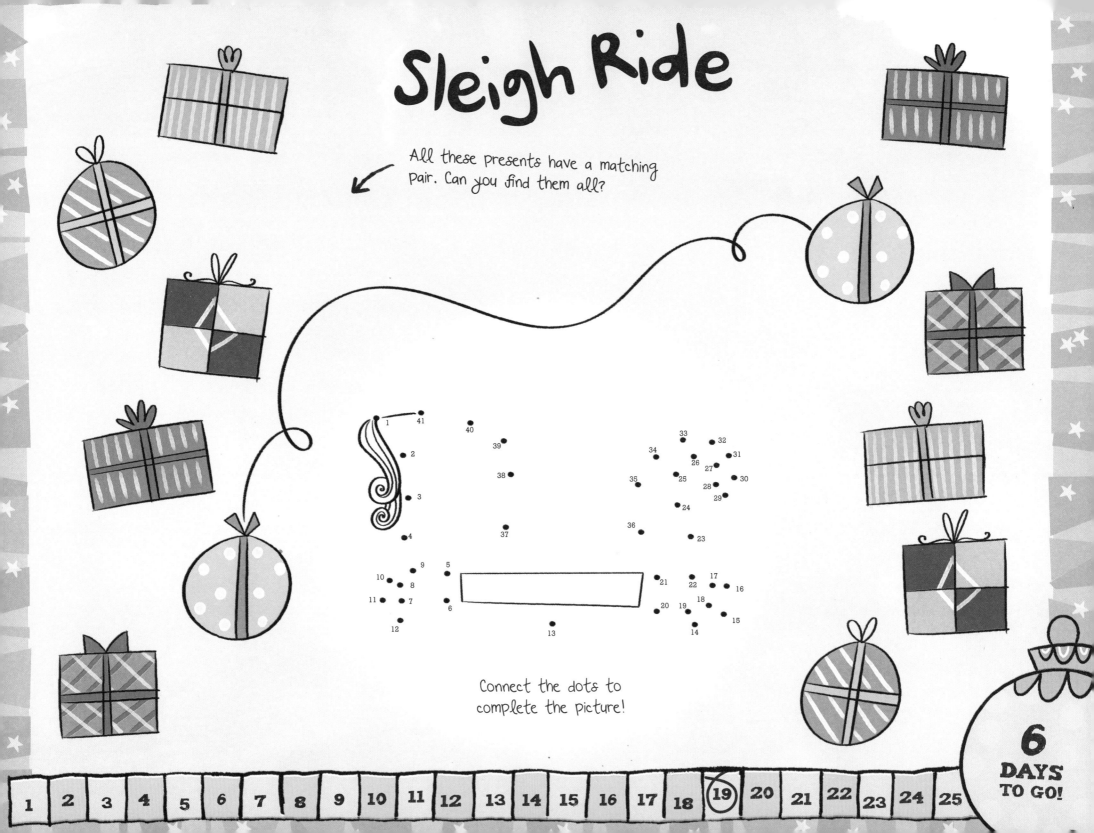

Connect the dots to complete the picture!

6 DAYS TO GO!

1 2 3 4 5 6 7 8 9 10 11 12 13 14 15 16 17 18 19 20 21 22 23 24 25

# Hang your Stockings

Design stockings for your friends and family!

Now copy your stockings in a lovely spot on the mantelpiece! Don't forget to write your and your family members' names on them.

**5 DAYS TO GO!**

| 1 | 2 | 3 | 4 | 5 | 6 | 7 | 8 | 9 | 10 | 11 | 12 | 13 | 14 | 15 | 16 | 17 | 18 | 19 | 20 | 21 | 22 | 23 | 24 | 25 |

# Odd One Out

Can you find the matching pairs (and the odd one out) in each of these puzzles?

1.

2.

3.

4.

5.

# Help Santa Claus

Santa Claus needs to pick up all the presents in the maze before finding his way to his sleigh! Can you help him?

It's time for Santa to get ready for the big night! Draw and color in his famous suit.

| 1 | 2 | 3 | 4 | 5 | 6 | 7 | 8 | 9 | 10 | 11 | 12 | 13 | 14 | 15 | 16 | 17 | 18 | 19 | 20 | 21 | 22 | 23 | 24 | 25 |
|---|---|---|---|---|---|---|---|---|----|----|----|----|----|----|----|----|----|----|----|----|----|----|----|----|

**4 DAYS TO GO!**

# Around the World

Here are some fun Christmas traditions from around the world.

Santa zooms across the whole planet! Mark all the continents on his map.

In Australia, it is summer when Christmas comes around. For those living near the beach it's a tradition to hit the waves on Christmas day and sometimes have a barbecue!

In the UK and USA, some families decorate their houses with lots of twinkling Christmas lights! They often leave a charity collection box outside for people who admire the house.

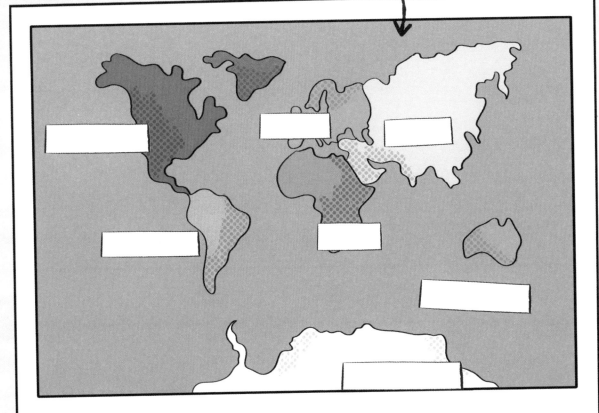

Children in Iceland put shoes on their windowsill to be filled with goodies on Christmas Eve!

Watch out if you have a Christmas pudding in Scotland! Traditional clootie dumpling is often filled with coins or silver charms for good luck!

In Norway, children leave out porridge for a creature called Jul Nisse. If they forget, he might play tricks on them!

| 1 | 2 | 3 | 4 | 5 | 6 | 7 | 8 | 9 | 10 | 11 | 12 | 13 | 14 | 15 | 16 | 17 | 18 | 19 | 20 | 21 | 22 | 23 | 24 | 25 |
|---|---|---|---|---|---|---|---|---|----|----|----|----|----|----|----|----|----|----|----|----|----|----|----|----|

**3 DAYS TO GO!**

# Merry Christmas

Santa Claus has to say "Merry Christmas" in a lot of different languages around the world. Connect the language he is speaking with the flag of the country he is in!

France

Sweden

Spain

Germany

Italy

Buon Natale!

Fröhliche weihnachten!

Joyeux Noël!

¡Feliz Navidad!

God Jul!

Design your own flag for Christmas!

# Fabulous Food

Can you find everything on the shopping list? Check off each item as you go!

Yum! Can you spot the four differences between these delicious Christmas dinners?

- ☐ Candies
- ☐ Gingerbread men
- ☐ Candy canes
- ☐ Carrots
- ☐ Brussels sprouts
- ☐ Chocolate
- ☐ Walnuts
- ☐ Orange juice

Answers: These items are missing from the second plate: brussels sprout, sausage, carrot, turkey thigh

1 2 3 4 5 6 7 8 9 10 11 12 13 14 15 16 17 18 19 20 21 22 (23) 24 25

**2 DAYS TO GO!**

# Christmas Popper

See if you can work out the punch lines to these Christmas popper jokes. If you don't know them, then make up your own (they might be funnier than the originals!).

1. Why are Christmas trees so bad at sewing? Because they always drop their:

_____

2. What do you get when you cross a vampire and a snowman?

_____

3. How do snowmen travel? They ride on:

_____

4. What do you get if you eat too many Christmas decorations?

_____

5. Who delivers Christmas presents to all the animals? Santa:

_____

6. What's the best thing to put in a Christmas cake? Your:

_____

↑
Draw your dream Christmas popper prize coming out of this popper!

Answers: 1. Needles, 2. Frostbite, 3. Icicles, 4. Tinselitis, 5. Paws, 6. Teeth.

| 1 | 2 | 3 | 4 | 5 | 6 | 7 | 8 | 9 | 10 | 11 | 12 | 13 | 14 | 15 | 16 | 17 | 18 | 19 | 20 | 21 | 22 | 23 | 24 | 25 |
|---|---|---|---|---|---|---|---|---|----|----|----|----|----|----|----|----|----|----|----|----|----|----|----|----|

**1 DAY TO GO!**

# It's Christmas Day

I got up at ___ am.

**MERRY CHRISTMAS!** The day has finally arrived. It's time to relax and enjoy it! Fill in all the fun things you've done so far, and everything you're going to do later.

The **BEST GIFT** I've got so far is _____ _____

The best gift someone else got was _____ _____ and I've had _____ for breakfast!

Have you had any **CANDIES** or chocolate yet?

Of course! ☐

Not yet! ☐

Draw your **FANTASY** Christmas dinner here! You never know, you might just get it! (But probably not!)

The **FUNNIEST** thing that's happened so far is _____

Later on we're going to _____ _____

I'm going to stay up until _____ tonight!

Merry Christmas!

| 1 | 2 | 3 | 4 | 5 | 6 | 7 | 8 | 9 | 10 | 11 | 12 | 13 | 14 | 15 | 16 | 17 | 18 | 19 | 20 | 21 | 22 | 23 | 24 | 25 |

# Boxing Day

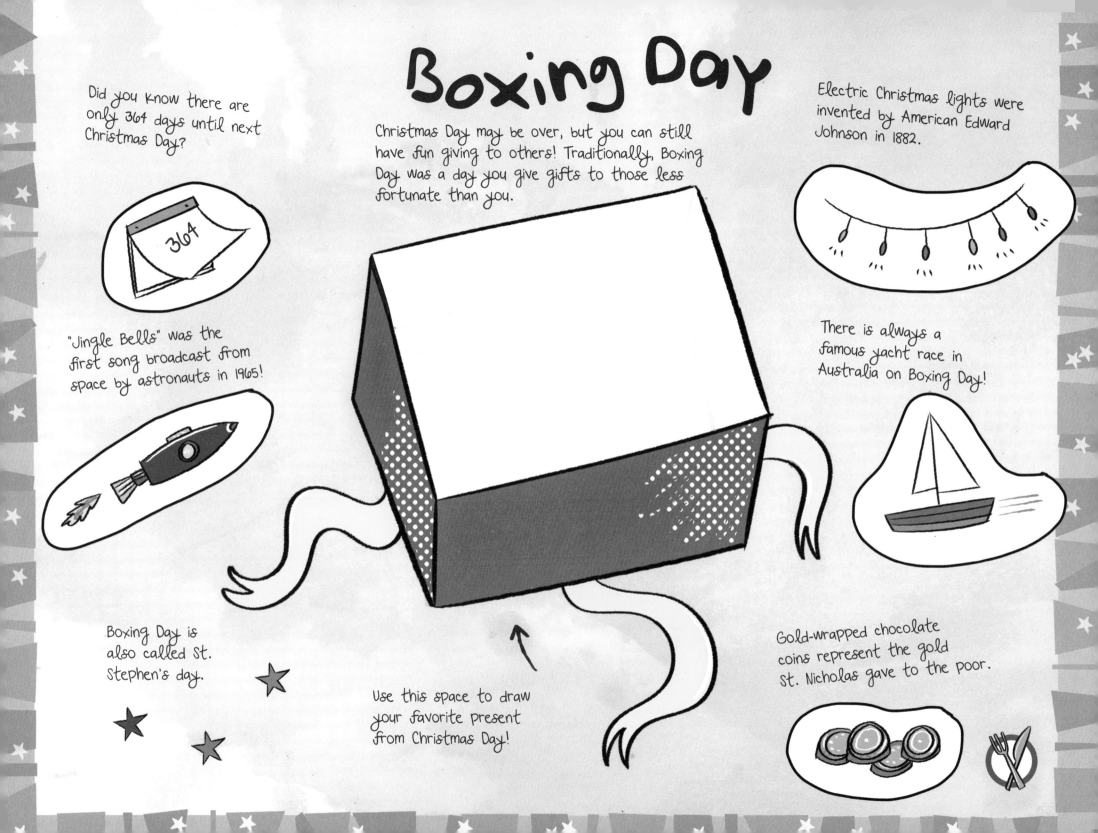

Did you know there are only 364 days until next Christmas Day?

Christmas Day may be over, but you can still have fun giving to others! Traditionally, Boxing Day was a day you give gifts to those less fortunate than you.

Electric Christmas lights were invented by American Edward Johnson in 1882.

"Jingle Bells" was the first song broadcast from space by astronauts in 1965!

There is always a famous yacht race in Australia on Boxing Day!

Boxing Day is also called St. Stephen's day.

Use this space to draw your favorite present from Christmas Day!

Gold-wrapped chocolate coins represent the gold St. Nicholas gave to the poor.